Refusing to Grow III

The Dean who was promoted for losing
her institute's accreditation.

A. Ruben

Printed in the United States of America.

Refusing to Grow 3: the Dean who was promoted for losing her institute's accreditation. / Ruben

ISBN: 978-0-9754590-4-1

Ickynicks Publishing

Front Cover by Adam Zillins

The following story is based upon actual events and people. However the timeline of events has been compressed and edited to accommodate the story and its characters. Any similarity of dramatized characters, incidents, companies, or attributes to any actual person, living or dead, or to any actual event or to any existing organization is entirely coincidental and unintentional.

Note to the Reader

The following chronological series of semi-disconnected incidents are based on true events and characters, which capture certain personalities perhaps too ridiculous to imagine. Yet, they are neither exaggerations nor embellishments.

Preface

Before Cleveland or LA, young Arthur first sought to further his education by pursuing a master's degree. Yet, amidst ethical conflict, racism and depravity, his education was unexpectedly cut short with nothing to show for it except student debt.

Accused of academic dishonesty, he was neither expected to triumph nor create such upheaval. Instead, he was simply expected to go quietly into the night, accepting his unfortunate circumstances as fate. But he absolved his name from perseverance and persistence, and as a result scores of resignations and dismissals followed.

Sadly, he learned that hard work is not always rewarded as he was taught as a child. Instead, it can stand out or catch the envy of others seeking the limelight; when he finally achieved his dream job of teaching it came at the expense of tax dollars, and for the first time in his life Arthur restrained himself from going above and beyond.

Cast of Characters:

Arthur – An optimistic and aspiring student, he will exceed his academic expectations. Yet, instead of reward he will be accused of academic dishonesty.

Dr. Hayword – The Dean, she will deny Arthur assistance in appealing his case as well as refuse any faculty in helping him.

Dr. Hollis – Academic Supervisor to Arthur, she will deny him help as well as assume an unethical role of serving as Chair of the Ethics Committee, which will investigate the charges against him.

The Board of Trustees / The Board – Overseeing budgetary decisions of the institution, the chair and board members will transition from a policy of expansion to one of slowing down and assessing growth.

Dr. Koleman – An Accreditation Consultant, he will be hired by the institute to evaluate its curriculum and program in order to determine its eligibility for advanced accreditation. After Arthur's dismissal however, he will neither renew his contract nor award the institute accreditation.

Stephanie – Chief Director as well as Arthur's internship supervisor, she will bring trumped-up charges against him, but will later be dismissed when the charges are proven unfounded.

Dr. Sobrick – A close associate with Stephanie, he will support her allegations against Arthur until she is dismissed.

Yolanda / "Mama Bear" – Records Manager, she will assist Arthur at his internship as well as prove indispensable in helping him appeal his case.

Acknowledgements

The author wishes to thank the following for their support, Lynn, Marilyn, Alex, Sara, Rochelle and Mike. Thank you very much for your assistance in making this work possible.

The following is based on a true story.

Contents

The Faculty

Chapter 1

Welcome Day

The warm rays of sunlight illuminated the grand lobby as new students passed into the foyer to begin their orientation. Eager to start their advanced education, they were greeted by faculty as well as the Dean, Dr. Hayword. She reached out and shook everyone's hand with a smile, thanking each one for applying. One of those hands belonged to a young man named Arthur, who thanked her for the opportunity.

After working hard in his undergraduate, he was excited to begin his advanced studies in a profession that he hoped would help others. Like others, he was eager, optimistic, and ready to tackle the challenges ahead; he had worked three jobs while earning his Bachelor's, and felt prepared to work hard again.

A. Ruben

As students filed in, starting up conversations and asking questions, Arthur looked around at the grand lobby. Around the room exhibited the history of the institute, including a showcase of landmark dates and pictures. One was a black and white photograph of a man digging the first hole at its founding. Arthur smiled, relating to it; he too felt he was beginning, setting the foundation of his career. Other exhibits lauded an encouraging list of graduates over the decades as well as distinguished awards the institute had won. The more Arthur read the more he felt sure about this institution.

Helping others had always been a part of him. Once in his youth, he spent an entire snow-day off from school helping a neighbor dig his car out. He also volunteered at soup kitchens, nursing homes, and even aided an elderly neighbor with her yard work. Even in grade school he had defended others against bullies, and now he had an opportunity unlike any other to advance his education and pave a future that would help others.

As the room came alive with lively discussions and explorations of curiosities, Arthur smiled joyfully, happy to be here. He had been accepted at other institutions, but had chosen this one; one university had even assembled his committee and chair in advance notice, an almost unheard of act.

But of all the institutions he had visited he felt this was the right place for him. As the Dean took the microphone he listened with eagerness.

Chapter 2

The Dean

Dr. Hayword prided herself on embodying the vision of the institution, which was to become an international leader in graduate education; every hand she shook was one more budding figure to that goal.

"Thank you everyone for choosing to be here," she said, smiling as she spoke into the microphone. "I am so thrilled to see you so excited for this year, and as you walk around I want to thank you for preparing to launch yourselves into a career that will take you to new experiences; and which will ultimately help us realize our dream: that success lies in each and every one of us."

She paused briefly and walked over to a laptop to hit the play button. At once, a slideshow began. Projected on a large screen on the wall it was titled, *Every One of Us* and it boasted the institute's graduates in all areas of the community, from hospitals to businesses to higher education teaching to private business.

"I cannot express my humble thanks and joy to see you here," she said passionately. "And I want to add that your connection with us is so important. Each of you will have a place in our history, whether as an alumni, or as a supporter of our growth; your contributions to this school are a living legacy to all those who follow in your footsteps. This year marks the largest group of incoming students to our program, and I am so pleased set the tone of your educational experience. I know that it is with both creativity and great determination that we will carry forward the values of learning and education as we progress into the months ahead."

Then she introduced the faculty and concluded her speech. "And as I look out at every one of you, I see a richer history come alive. I see accomplished goals and dreams realized. And I see so many of you playing a part in helping this wonderful place grow."

As Dean of Academic Affairs, Dr. Hayword had had a successful tenure so far. Under her leadership, academic achievement and admissions had risen, with the latter up by 130%. Even more complimenting was the number of graduates every year. It was no surprise then that the Board of Trustees approved her nearly every decision, including an increase in faculty as well as the all-important hire of Dr. Koleman:

With over twenty-five years of experience, Dr. Koleman was as much a pioneer in research as he was a leading voice in his field. Having served as program director and chair on several committees, his reputation was well established in the academic community. Although a modest man, his humility belied his hurried nature. As someone from the East Coast, he was accustomed to being "on the go," and often forgot to tuck his shirt in. He talked fast, and moved with a purpose wherever he went.

Flown across the country to serve on the faculty, he accepted their offer, but only after securing the role as Chair of Graduate Studies as well as a substantial compensation salary to which the Board had initially hesitated. Yet, owing to his secondary role as an evaluator for advanced accreditation they acquiesced.

For everyone, the future was as bright and optimistic as anyone could expect then; students were elated to start, the Board eagerly awaited its endorsement, and faculty were excited to begin educating. Few if any realized what would soon unfold.

<u>Chapter 3</u>

The Apple Giver

In addition to the electricity of hiring Dr. Koleman, the Board was also ecstatic to bring aboard Dr. Sobrick, whose network was as impressive as his résumé. Upon his hire, Dr. Sobrick at once arranged a series of seminars and workshops at a national convention in order to showcase the institution; the Dean overwhelmingly approved the act, noting it as a "polished tribute to our values and mission."

Reporting on his successes to the Board, Dr. Hayword further added his openness to the institution's principles. "It is pleasing to see such receptivity to our ideas." But Dr. Sobrick had only just begun. Setting up additional workshops, he presented at an international conference a few weeks later, and once again curried favor with the institution by commending its founding leaders.

"There is no doubt in my mind that he will further

our direction," she said. The Board agreed; despite the overbearing expenditures of his productions, the chair approved his endeavors.

"Promoting discussion of our philosophies is just as important as bringing in new students," the chair replied, sharing her enthusiasm. The two were old friends, and he was happy to support her.

Chapter 4

A Lesson in Ethics

Outside of the institute, was a sculpture garden named in Dr. Hayword's honor. As a patron of the arts, she enjoyed art for its beauty, but also its inspiration. In her office was a sculpted eagle set eternally in launch, its wings outspread and beak cawing.

* * * * * * * *

A few days after orientation, Arthur met with Dr. Hollis. "I have scheduled your internship to begin next week," she said, giving him the name of his site supervisor, Stephanie. "She will monitor your progress there, and I will follow your progress here."

A reserved woman, Dr. Hollis always carried a look of trepidation about her, as though she was holding onto a deep, dark secret that she feared others might discover.

Short and withdrawn, her confidence was only buoyed whenever she wore business attire, which is perhaps why she dreaded casual Fridays just as much as the annual faculty-student picnic, which she declined to attend every year. She approached everyone with mistrust and caution, wary to extend help or receive it; she favored retreat over conflict, regardless of morality and instead harboring a deep sense of self-preservation that ran through her core.

And although she enjoyed teaching, she neither strayed from her lectures into tangent discussions of interest nor moved away from her podium; she enjoyed the company of students, but feared strangers, and so struggled in the early parts of the semester. She walked gingerly down the hallways, hastening her step as much as picking her feet up in case she needed to extract herself from imminent danger; she suspected the walls had eyes and ears.

And whenever by the opposite sex passed by, she hugged the wall. Though neither married nor eager to speak of marriage, she reframed from discussing it or being in the presence of someone recently engaged; she once alluded to a significant other, but made no mention of it further.

In the break room, she spoke of love in distant metaphors, implying it, but refraining from using the word or any reference to it; although she may have had someone close to her heart, she neither would admit it publicly nor offer a name. She was a quiet woman that enjoyed the company of women; for whatever reason, men unsettled her, and she neither received their advances nor their presence. She preferred the homogenous company of others, easing back to a glass of wine, and reveling in such topics as shopping or suburban gossip.

Only in the presence of her closest friends did she reveal herself, unlocking the safe of her most inner desires, unearthing an entirely different woman than the world knew. Recanting her modesty, she shared her most erotic fantasies of bondage, a black corset wrapped around a tight cavity, a pair of high heels and a riding crop- tapping ever so rigorously against her soft behind. She enjoyed restraints, preferring cuffs to rope, but had experimented with ankle as well as wrists; the bar and cuff had been tried, but she enjoyed being subdued without obstacle; her desired mistress was a dirty blonde, unashamed and fearless.

She admitted to being anything but domestic in the moonlight. Untamed and craving punishment, she sought out any woman of similar athletic build who could prolong her bliss, desiring deep penetration from behind most of all.

Only in private did she ever disclose her intimate

fantasies, but once or twice she erred at the institute; forgetting her surroundings, she entreated her erotism before realizing where she was, and retreating to her office in haste for fear of being discovered. She hid herself, and her true feelings. She was woman in love with other women, but society had not yet embraced homosexuality; gay marriage was still illegal at the federal level, and it was not yet a socially acceptable norm.

And so she hid, but not from potential lovers. For them she threw out cues, subtle hints of her sexual orientation, such as her short hair, which she excused as easier to maintain when questioned about it.

She supervised students as an advisor, including Arthur, but also chaired the Ethics Committee, perhaps as a way to pepper away any rumors or simply to shield the truth from her own conscious. Either way, she neither came out of the closet nor praised those that did. In fact, she scorned those that did come out, ridiculing them as well as damning them; whether ashamed of herself or simply fearing persecution by others if discovered, she neither supported those who dared to risk it all, or even felt they were worthy of Paradise.

Moreover, she admonished any pride news or events happening in the public, particularly parades, avoiding any detection whenever possible, even at the risk of ostracism; she steered clear of social movements as she did politics, often slipping into sheep's skin as she sided with protestors against homosexuality. It broke her heart, but she could not risk being discovered lest she lose her job, her reputation, and perhaps even more her friends and family.

And yet, she kept five separate colored pens on her desk, carefully aligned to resemble a rainbow; she was a subtle woman. A quiet woman. A lesbian. Proud, but shamed.

Chapter 5

Counting Every Penny

"Words cannot express the awakening of my heart," Dr. Hayword said to the Board. They had just approved her nominees. "I feel my spirit evoked." Her words were as extravagant as the sculpture pieces in her office- but statues can't forge their own opinions. And so, she did her best to keep the Board in the dark, believing in her vision only.

* * * * * * * *

Arthur was still in debt for his bachelor's degree, despite having worked three jobs. Nevertheless, he was willing to take on more debt if it meant a promising future. At a cost of $460 per credit hour, his tuition came to almost $25,000 a year. This also included fees, such as $100 for using the electrical outlets in the building as well as with one-on-one meetings with Dr. Hollis.

Taking additional loan money for room and board, he found an apartment that should have been earmarked for demolition. His apartment was barren, but not for want of furniture: the crunching under his foot of whatever crawled under the carpet was too repulsive. And so, he limited himself to the tile floor of the kitchen and bathroom and his room.

Across the street sat a bank with bars on its windows, and a bulletproof countertop window inside; nearby was an abandoned shopping center, often with two cars pulling up beside one another in the back lot. No doubt just to chat. Beside the bank was a grocery store that boasted security cameras, and yet a customer had to beat back an assailant right outside the exit door; he tried to take her purse, but grabbed the milk instead. A block away, a robbed pharmacy simply forwent cameras and just started carrying a shotgun.

At night, Arthur could hear drive-by shootings as well as curses and taunts. At first, he was shaken by it, seeking shelter in his bathtub, but after awhile he just accepted it as his nightly ritual, and often fell asleep to it. His one neighbor upstairs was always high, and the once across the hall was always stirring together spices and pork, making the air an olfactory tangle of jambalaya and marijuana.

A. Ruben

And everyday Arthur left wearing a tie, which his sous-chef neighbor once remarked as unusual for someone going into the ghetto. "Oh baby, that is a noose," she said. "But boy do you look handsome. I know some pretty girl will find you, and just eat you up."

Chapter 6

The Internship

Two blocks down from his apartment was a donut shop that police enjoyed every morning at 6 am. One time it was robbed just beforehand, and the thief, being intelligent as he was, walked out with the cash and a handful of donuts just as the officers were walking in.

* * * * * * * *

At his internship, Stephanie greeted Arthur with a firm handshake. She was eager to get started just as much as he was. Located in an inner-city neighborhood, the area had seen better days: the homes were clearly from a golden age that time forgot, and potholes now lined the streets like mortar holes in a war zone. Scattered and abandoned, some homes were even burned out simply left to rot; two homes beside the facility were in just disrepair that homeless people even refused to sleep there. Everywhere, gang markings and graffiti covered the neighborhood.

"This isn't a great place," she said, "but it's the neighborhood we have to work with, and I hope with your help we can do that." But her optimism belied the sharpness in her voice. Cunning, shrewd, and authoritative, her reputation preceded her when she had transferred to the facility four years ago; neither the staff nor the management team were excited about her transfer, and her unfriendly demeanor did nothing to help.

Disparagingly nicknamed, "She-Boss," she neither complimented nor recognized achievement. Far from caring or amiable, her conversations were a series of directives, issued with as little sympathy as possible; she neither asked about someone's day nor engaged in friendly discourse with those outside of her race.

A block of ice, she treated others inhospitably, belittling minorities like second-class citizens, and regularly dismissing their sense of humanity as nothing more than a pipedream. "Many of these people need a helping hand," she said, often noting that the color of her skin inherently burdened her with the responsibility of helping those unable to help themselves. "Not everyone is as fortunate as you and I, and so we must help them."

Whereas others might debate welfare on an economic level or fiscal accountability, she viewed it as a racial responsibility, insisting it was necessary to aid those less fortunate, and by that she meant less superior. She neither claimed to be a racist nor pass judgment, but her speech was always bigoted, ranking Whites as superior to all others. And too often religion was supplemented to support her argument. "Not everybody was created equally. Some were born less fortunate, and so it is our duty to provide for them."

To those that accused her of racism, she simply shielded herself with a shroud of morality. "To do my job right means to be direct sometimes," she once defended, "but it is always with the utmost intentions to help others less fortunate." Likened to a plantation owner's wife, she embraced naivety in her bigotry, asserting whatever she said or did was "right and just," and important in "redirecting misguidance." In four years, she dismissed nearly two-dozen people.

"How we help others is a lot like how we raise children," she once said. "There needs to be defined lines." She once terminated a staff member for speaking out of turn.

Chapter 7

Deep Roots

The facility employed nearly 350 people as staff members, managers, and directors. Each department had at least three managers and roughly two-dozen staff members; supervising all of them was Stephanie, who reported to the facility's CEO.

"Success begins with leadership," she once said, asserting her slanted philosophy of unlocking human potential. "By leading others towards a more productive and meaningful life, we can inspire action that results in rebuilding lives and restoring dignity." And yet, not one of her fourteen directors was a minority.

In the past, the administration had been heterogeneous, but that changed when she came aboard; confronted by allegations, she simply asserted that only the most suitable applicants had been selected for the positions.

But whereas racism was shuffled under the rug, it was blatantly open in the public. In one instance, Arthur went to eat at a local fast food restaurant and the white manager manning the cash register flagrantly bypassed four others in front of him, who happened to be minorities. Appalled, he left instead. In another instance, his meal was brought ahead of a Black couple that had been seated much longer than he. He refused to eat until they had their food. But yet another time, a manager politely informed a family of four that he had no open tables, and yet he had just combined two small tables for a White family of four.

Arthur was simply appalled. How could this still be happening in the 21st Century? But Stephanie felt it was not only understandable but also a perpetual part of society.

"The only way to overcome it is not through laws," she said, "but by embracing it, and accepting what is and what will always be." She saw racism as an inherent part of civilization as well as an inevitable social issue that arose out of the sentiment of the minority. "These people will often not realize that they are in need of help, and so it behooves us to take action and support them, however it is we can."

She saw the White race as the steward of civilization. "There are those that can and those that can't," she frequently said, believing there was a parallel between the White race and its responsibility of caring for other races.

"Just look at the demographics," she said, quoting the bible, too often referencing the story of Joseph and how he had to care for his brothers when they came to Egypt. "Some people simply can't take care of themselves."

Moreover, she further saw racism as a manufactured by-product of minorities, noting that those who required help to survive always seemed to covet some small amount of jealously from those who could; she often lamented that "these people" failed then to recognize the steadfast devotion and commitment of others to help them meet their basic human needs. In one instance, she referred to statistics, noting that in cases of discrimination the persons involved often demanded compensation, but were already receiving welfare assistance. "Some people just don't know how to say thank you."

And it was this in mind that structured her way of thinking and guided her decision-making process. She was resolved in the notion that it was her social obligation as a member of the White race to guide those less fortunate than herself in reaching what limited potential they could ever hope to achieve in this world; and as the core values of the facility were about empowering others, she furthermore believed that she was adhering to those: that despite barriers she believed people could make an effort.

"Someone has to be willing to try," she said, "and we have to be there to help him or her." And yet, she recognized the existence of a racial glass ceiling. For when Arthur suggested the possibility of a minority becoming President of the US one day; this was long before President Obama He might have well as said the moon was going to crash into Earth.

She just shook her head, and politely dismissed it as unrealistic. "These people need our help. They can achieve some measure of standing, but let's not get carried away. There will never be a Black President."

Chapter 8

The Big House

To the Dean's enthusiasm, the Board approved the hire of a new Vice President of Administration, who was to report to her directly. "I am so heartened by the spirit evident in this group," she said.

* * * * * * * *

The facility had four levels, and employees crudely referred to the fourth floor as the "Big House," since it was where Stephanie's office was located. There racism was as paramount as discipline: everyone did as he or she was told, and every task was accepted with a "yes, ma'am." Any lax was met with swift retribution, and employees often referred to receiving her castigations as, "being whipped."

Whereas Stephanie frequently boasted that the facility had a cordial work environment, the reality was that hospitality was nothing more than an extension of prejudice. It was not only mandatory but unfortunately weighed to one side: the middle of the hallway was reserved for directors, and employees were required to say good morning to their bosses.

"Morning ma'am."

"Good morning to you too."

Being polite was simply another act of submission as neither Stephanie nor her directors offered the greeting first. Moreover, it fell in line with her slanted policies, which not only caused discomfort but also disenfranchisement.

In one such policy, employees were required to remain hospitable at all times, even when receiving a reprimand. "Thank you, ma'am," or "thank you, sir," was as expected as a morning welcome. After all, as Stephanie reasoned, courtesy was a measure of civilization. How else could the lowly be expected to rise?

And thus, the fourth floor had the highest expectations. Regimented as well as rigorous, it was the most compliant. But its silence belied the hustle and flow of every worker on that floor, who feared the "she-boss" peeking over their shoulder.

Chapter 9

Yolanda

Ironically, across from Stephanie's office was a flagrant contradiction to her racial philosophy. Her name was Yolanda, and she was not only the highest-ranking minority at the facility but also her equal since they both reported to the CEO.

Yolanda neither took orders from Stephanie nor harbored any indignant opinions of her despite her slanted views on race. Although she didn't approve of her policies, she neither interjected nor demeaned the woman. Instead, she counseled advice, urging prudence and compliance for the greater good. "Oh honey, it is about survival," she said to one employee who had become fed up.

But by no means was Yolanda a coward or pacifist. Although she revered past and present leaders in her community, such as Martin Luther King Jr. and Malcolm X, her experiences in life had taught her the value of vigilance and integration.

Whereas others protested, pointing out the inequities within society, she advanced herself by embracing those inequities. As she once explained to Arthur, she took her lesson from Benjamin Franklin, who she read about as a little girl. Since the French saw him a certain way he simply embraced it instead of protesting that perspective. As a result he earned their audience as well as an alliance between France and the fledging new United States.

"Life isn't equal, but it's about how you respond to those equalities that sets you apart from others," she said.

As the highest minority in the facility, she now used her power and authority to balance the scale. She often walked down the middle of the hallway. But it was religion that truly gave her strength. Like others, she too had experienced prejudice and discrimination, including horrific bigotry upon her late husband. Early in their relationship, three men had assailed him while they were on a date. He had tried to defend her, but was overpowered and beaten to near death. She cried at nights when she remembered it, cherishing his bravery, but it was her children that she felt the most pain.

A. Ruben

She forgave the world, but did not forget. When her son came of age he was belittled and told to go back to doing manual labor, because "that's what his kind was best at."

Sadly, it was only the beginning of his exposure to bigotry. Nevertheless, he eventually went to medical school and became a doctor. But it grieved her heart even more when she overheard two nurses refer to her daughter's new baby as "just another welfare statistic." Walking up to them she took out her organ donor's card.

"I've given so much to this world and to my family," she said, looking at them in disgust. "And I pray that when I die someone in your family or someone dear to you may be grateful enough to have received my final gift."

Chapter 10

Reverence

Ingratiated with the nickname, "Mama Bear," Yolanda helped anybody with an issue or question. She looked out for everyone as though they were her own children.

"Now you just be careful," she warned Arthur. "I don't want to see you get hurt." After twenty-nine years of service, she was more than knowledgeable. She was respected. Even the directors paid her reverence, accepting not only instructions from her, but also taking example from her and disobeying some of Stephanie's policies, such as the hallway "courtesy." Many gave employees the right-of-way, and even greeted them in the morning.

Moreover, they also helped her in any way they could, often putting her vender orders before Stephanie's. "If there's anything else I can help with," one said to her. "Just let me know." As it were, most if not all preferred her leadership to the she-boss.

And that fact wasn't lost on Stephanie, who felt so offended that she tried on several occasions to get her terminated, but the CEO repeatedly found her to be too indispensable to dismiss. Moreover, he applauded her efforts and encouraged Stephanie to do likewise; when she insisted that Yolanda be moved to another floor, he denied her request and instead asked her to meet with Yolanda weekly to improve the overall operation of the facility.

And so with deep regret and reluctance, Stephanie obliged, resenting not only the fact that her racial opinion of the world was challenged weekly, but also that her directors failed to share her views.

Chapter 11

Hours and Files

"Now you watch yourself sweetie," Yolanda said to Arthur as she left for the night. "It's a dangerous world out there, and I'm going home to make biscuits and a mean chili." She loved to cook, and everyone looked forward to her bringing something in; even Stephanie admittedly agreed it was good.

* * * * * * * *

As per Stephanie's instruction, Arthur recorded his hours at his internship and so every time he entered or left he signed in and out, even during lunch. Although he often brought his own lunch, Stephanie would occasionally send him out to get her something, and he was happy to oblige.

A. Ruben

Since his internship required 500 hours for completion, and each semester mandated a minimum record of 167 hours, he kept track of his hours, and only those approved by Stephanie; not everything could be counted, and so he took special care to count his hours carefully.

In addition to meeting with Stephanie and reviewing his hours, he also received files from her on his clients. Although a student, part of his internship included the experience of serving as a professional with actual clients; following the appointment, he then reviewed their cases with Stephanie before issuing a diagnosis.

"Every week I will give you new files," she said to him. "I want you to review them before meeting with the client, and then afterwards we will discuss them. Furthermore, I want you to take the files home and study them," she added. "Because there is absolutely no excuse for not being aware of the client's conditions before meeting with him or her."

Chapter 12

Networking

When the Board voted to hire four more staff members, Dr. Hayword gave them her thanks. "The message that students continue to hear is our promise of a bright future for them."

* * * * * * * *

Yolanda was as much a matriarchal figurehead in the office as she was in her community. In addition to being sought after for parental guidance by other parents, she also became a godmother to many households. A bastion of morality, she rooted right and wrong into the young ones of her community as well as set high expectations by being the example:

A. Ruben

A religious woman, she cherished the Bible for its principles of duty and devotion. "We are all God's children," she told Arthur. "Now that doesn't mean we all share in the same faiths or views, but it does mean we all have to learn to get along with one another; one day we will all have to report to the same parent upstairs."

But although she was pious, she rarely quoted the Bible and instead lived by its canon, preferring to practice what she believed rather than simply preach it; even in the face of blatant depravity, she stood her ground as was the case when a couple of local gang members tried to mug her. "You may take from me, but only when I'm cold and dead and I have no intention of that today!" One of the members recognized her and apologized immensely.

"Please don't tell my mother. She'd die if she knew," he begged.

"You reap what you sow. If I don't help you then who will?"

"Oh shit," he said, to which she snapped her fingers at him. "Oh sorry."

"Now run along, and the next time I see you I better see you in better clothes. Get them washed, you hear?"

"Yes ma'am."

"Now run along."

Revered by adults as well as children, she corrected as she saw fit, but always with a degree of balance and respect. She never undermined a parent or belittled a teenager. "I have children of my own you know," she said, recognizing the sensitivity among teenagers, especially when it came to matters of reputation: the gang member above was later encouraged by her to volunteer at the community center and soon after recruited more of his friends to spend the day with her and others. "Darling, you are now as much a part of my family as my own children," she said.

She helped others in any way that she could, whether it was at the soup kitchen or being firm in correcting bad manners. She neither tolerated churlish behavior nor ignorance. "This world will give you nothing," she snapped at a boisterous boy once, whose vulgarity and aggression in public was creating an unsettling feeling among others. "Now you better shape up and learn how to plant those feet mister, because that mouth goes shut right now and the next words I want to hear out of you are apologies and what you can do to help out around here!"

At the office, she also helped out however she could, including introducing Arthur to every director and manager. They were happy to meet him and welcomed his questions.

"I'd have to say that the toughest part of my job is staying within budget," said one director. "Unlike the private sector, we are non-profit and so we operate on state grants and donations. The more money we have of course the more services we can offer."

Each director had something different to share, but they all agreed on one thing, budgets. "There are so many needs in our community, but with limited funds it's hard to meet those needs. That's why the private sector has it so good. They can make as much money as they want," said one.

As Arthur listened, they opened up to him, sharing their passions as well as their trials and tribulations. "But my door is always open for you," they said, welcoming his curiosity; of all the interns they had ever had, few if any had interacted with them or shown such interest as Arthur. "Most of the time, my office is mistaken for the bathroom," one joked.

Chapter 13

Peculiar Statements

"Oh honey, you look so handsome today," Yolanda said to him. Unlike other interns who dressed casually to their internship, Arthur always wore a shirt and tie. "Now you go straight up to the third floor and meet that fine gentleman there," she said, ensuring he met a director at least once a day.

* * * * * * * * *

As Arthur met with his clients, he also met separately with Dr. Hollis and Stephanie to update them on his progress. But whereas the former often listened quietly and took notes the latter preferred to do the talking. "I also want you to buy this list of books," she said, giving him a laundry list. "And if you haven't already done so, I want you to start taking client files home and study them at night."

She also tried to share life lessons through stories that were both unsettling as they were awkward. One time, she told him how she almost left her child behind during a vacation in Mexico. "If I didn't have so much love for it, then I would have left it there," she said, eerily disregarding her own child's gender.

But even more disturbing was her arbitrary inquiry into Arthur's opinions and feelings in specific regards to others at the facility. In particular, she wanted to know how he felt about Yolanda as well as other staff members; over time however it seemed as if she was just fishing for information more than showing an interest in him as swift retribution followed to those he expressed had been most helpful to him and Yolanda. One time, she asked him if he had any biases, to which he replied no. "Do you believe you have any prejudices?" she asked, but he shook his head.

"I don't believe so."

"Well, what about if someone breaks into your home, or threatens your life? Wouldn't you feel something then?"

"In that scenario, I suppose so."

"See, so you do have prejudices," she said.

"In that extreme situation, yes."

"But it nevertheless is true."

He hesitantly agreed. "I guess."

46

Chapter 14

Timeliness

The existing librarian at the institute was replaced
with one more versed in technology. "We are updating
ourselves into the 21st Century," said the Dean excitedly. "We
need to be out there for everyone to see."

* * * * * * * *

In sharp contrast to Dr. Sobrick's energetic start, Dr.
Koleman began the year at a snail's pace, forgoing his usual
hurried manner for a more calculated approach.

Put in charge of the graduate program, he paced
himself by first becoming acquainted with the institute,
talking with faculty, and meeting with students; and against
his impulse to rush into things, he instead interlaced pace
with precision, recruiting half a dozen students to join him in

a research study. Whereas his colleague was busily presenting from one convention to the next, he instead simply set a date for the following year to present the group's findings at a conference. "Becoming someone is more important than being someone," he later said to Arthur.

"When you take the time, you do it right," he added, restraining his compulsion to rush into things. He wasn't much for slowing down, but nowadays he saw value in it; in his youth he felt as though he was falling behind others if he paused for even a second, but now the only thing creeping up on him was age.

"I can get more done in an hour than most people do in a day," he said, modestly boasting his talents. "But it's nothing to be proud of. It's just who I am." Slowing down wasn't much in his nature, but he recognized the need to adapt, especially when flying halfway across the country to a new environment where others didn't move as fast as he. "And a good teacher recognizes the needs of his students," he said. "So, if I have to slow down and explain something twice, then so be it. Learning is just that important."

He believed in complementing strengths and weaknesses in order to develop a more nurturing environment. As a result, his research team worked in pairs and met once a week to review their share; working together was as helpful as the pizza and beer. "When something has the time to grow," he said, "then it's worth ten times more."

Chapter 15

Solidarity

An administrative assistant position was created to assist the institute in implementing all aspects of programs and services. Instead, this new position became an executive assistant to the Dean.

* * * * * * * *

Nearly every day, Arthur was at his internship. When he wasn't there he was on campus studying, but as the workload increased from Stephanie he began to spend more time meeting with clients, reviewing his files and asking questions. As always, he tracked his time and kept record of it.

But as his expectations were raised so were concerns about unethical behavior. One day, Stephanie told him to begin issuing his diagnoses to clients much sooner. "You should know what condition they have by the end of the first session," she told him. It usually took him two or three sessions before to be absolutely sure. After all, he didn't want to misdiagnosis.

"Starting this week, I expect a diagnosis for each new client you have by Friday. If that means you need to study more or take files home then you better get to it."

But although he was willing to comply something troubled him. In the course of his inquiries with the directors, he had learned that the facility's budget came from not just state subsidies and donations but also insurance reimbursements. The latter earned by billing for diagnoses. Moreover, not all diagnoses were reimbursed, which further bothered him since Stephanie had instructed him to diagnosis only with those that the insurance company would reimburse. She referred to it as "the approved list."

Furthermore, when he questioned it a few days later he was told misdiagnosing didn't matter. "It doesn't matter if you're not sure what the person has. Just pick something on the list." Arthur found this to be highly unethical as well as immoral, but Stephanie simply reminded him that she had the power to sign off on his internship. "

A. Ruben

We get paid by issuing a diagnosis," she said, demanding his compliance. "The insurance companies don't care what the diagnosis is. They just want to see something that's on their list."

Nevertheless, Arthur couldn't oblige. It didn't feel right. Wasn't the point of issuing a diagnosis meant to help a person, not hinder him or her? Even more disturbing was how that misdiagnosis could affect that person's life altogether. And so after several restless nights he brought it to Dr. Hollis's attention, who told him to comply.

Chapter 16

Political Ties

Dr. Sobrick was pleased to hear that Stephanie was Arthur's site supervisor, as was the Dean. They both knew her. "She is wonderful," he said to Arthur, who did not realize that the three of them often had lunch together.

* * * * * * * *

Arthur was morally conflicted. He disapproved of the idea of mislabeling people, but his internship was in jeopardy if he did not comply. In addition to being told to do so by Stephanie, Dr. Hollis had further warned him that noncompliance would result in his expulsion from the academic program; unbeknownst to him, but she also ate lunch with the others on occasion.

A. Ruben

Deeply troubled and unable to sleep, he sought out help but unfortunately few if any were willing to counter Dr. Hollis. "She is your supervisor. So, you should be listening to her," he was told. Only Dr. Koleman questioned that.

"What's in your heart," he asked, when Arthur came to his door. As Arthur explained his dilemma, the man leaned back in his desk chair, unsettled by this revelation. "You must remember that whatever choices you make in life are yours to keep."

Arthur nodded. His past was a patchwork of outcomes of difficult choices. In one instance, he had served as a club's membership vice-president while finishing his bachelors. Yet instead of following his predecessors, he tried something new; instead of simply outreaching and marketing he held a series of seminars intended to be both interactive and fun. As a result, he attracted membership through word of mouth. Unfortunately, his pioneering success was both loathed and resented by the more traditional members of the club's leadership and they voted to replace him with someone more conventional. Within a short while the club's numbers were reduced to its original standing.

In another instance, his decisiveness saved other's, but not before a major confrontation. During a hiking expedition, the group's water supply ran extremely low. The only resupply point was a day's hike away and unfortunately over a mountain; it was either go around or take the grueling journey over it.

However, the group leader insisted they stay put, suggesting they march at night when it was cooler. Arthur disagreed. Of ten people there was only enough water for everyone to have a droplet; if they didn't go now then there would be nothing for later. Tensions suddenly mounted. At once the camp divided between those that wished to stay and rest and those wanting to press on. Those in support of Arthur prepared to leave, but were stopped by someone drawing a knife. With an escalating situation, Arthur asked to speak with the group leader alone, which gave everyone a chance to calm down. Seeing the situation turn, the leader finally consented and the group quenched their thirst several hours later on the other side of the mountain.

"So if you can live with this decision then go ahead," Dr. Koleman said. "But if there is anything that doesn't agree with you then you don't want to regret it."

Chapter 17

Swift Action

One day two men shot at each other outside of the facility. Neither hit the other, whether from poor aim or restraint, but when Arthur called the police he was put on hold.

* * * * * * * *

Unexpectedly, the Chair of the Board resigned to spend more time with his family as well as pursue other endeavors. At once, there was a stir of debate on which direction the board should take now. Should they continue a policy of growth or slow down and assess that growth? Dr. Hayword tried to argue for growth, reminding them that their efforts had indeed made a difference both among students as well as with the institute's reputation: its faculty was presenting at conventions, publishing, and every year the enrollment numbers were increasing; this year in particular was of importance for the expected advanced accreditation.

"I have no doubt we will get it," she said assuredly, "and it is owed to all of you."

And in anticipation of receiving it she told them she had already signed the institute up to attend the advanced accreditation convention the following year. "We will be there, because I can't see why that wouldn't be the case." In addition, Dr. Sobrick was to present there also.

The Board appreciated her proactive steps even if it was premature. Nevertheless, it voted in favor of prudence and cautioned her about making any future arrangements.

"At this time, I believe ensuring our house is in order should be our number one priority," said a board member, who was later elected as the new Chair.

Chapter 18

Reaching High

The new Chair's first order of business was tabling Dr. Hayword's request to fill the vacancy of Director of Development. It would remain vacant. This was a setback for Dr. Hayword, who was not accustomed to rejection, particularly when her vision of the institute had carried it so far.

* * * * * * * *

As the first semester came to a close, Arthur had recorded 332 hours at his internship. It was an impressive count, particularly because he was only expected to do about 167. But whereas other students had only gone once or twice a week he had gone nearly every day. In addition to learning more, he had also gained a plethora of experience in front of

clients as well as issuing diagnoses. Although he didn't agree
with Stephanie on all matters, he did appreciate her high level
of expectation.

Needless to say, Arthur felt quite proud of himself.
He had worked hard, learned a lot, and completed all of his
internship hours early so that he could focus on his thesis.
But as he entered Dr. Hollis's office to review his semester
she informed him that he was being accused of academic
dishonesty. Wait, what? His jaw dropped. That didn't make
any sense. But apparently- according to some faculty- it was
impossible for anyone to achieve such hours in a semester.
Thus, the only explanation for his hours was fabrication.

"But I was there nearly every day," he said, startled at
the news. He was lost for words. How could this be? He had
no idea. But as he would later discover the Dean- following
her rejection to fill a vacancy- Dr. Hayword had issued orders
to all staff that there were to be no inconsistencies- nothing
out of the ordinary- and if so, it was to be reported
immediately, quieted, and resolved quickly. This was
apparently her way of ensuring that the Board had no further
reason to reject any of her proposals: she had a vision for
growth and wished to avoid any discrepancies that might
postpone expansion; any issue was to be silenced and kept
away from the eyes and ears of the Board.

And thus it was that Arthur was being accused of dishonesty. No other student had achieved his number of hours, but then no other student had gone to their internship as often as him. A simple look at the records would have shown that he was telling the truth, but instead the institute drew a line in the sand, and refused to go back:

"But I have my hours recorded to prove it," he said, trying to argue his case. But Dr. Hollis dismissed his evidence, asserting that unless he appealed his case he would receive an incomplete for the entire semester. It was ridiculous. He had the hours on paper to exonerate him, and moreover his hours were signed and approved by Stephanie.

But Dr. Hollis continued to reject his evidence, informing him that if he did not appeal that he would be expelled from the institute.

Arthur sat back in his seat. This was not what he had expected when he walked in. He didn't understand why this was happening. What had he done to deserve this? "But I recorded everything I was told to record. I don't understand what I did wrong?"

Dr. Hollis lied. "I have reviewed your hours, and no, you did not record your hours as you were instructed."

What? That made no sense. Stephanie had walked him through how to fill out the paperwork, what duties were acceptable to record, and how to tally up his hours. How had he erred? Had Stephanie forgotten to tell him something?

"I will expect a revision of your hours by the end of this week," said Dr. Hollis, "As of this moment, you have zero hours for the semester, which constitutes a failure for the semester. If you wish to make up the hours you will need to speak with the registrar's office to sign up for an additional semester."

An extra semester? Arthur's eyes widened. This was bullshit. It had to be. At the cost he was paying for tuition he was already in debt up to his eyeballs, and now all of his hard work was for nothing. This was ridiculous. He had gone above and beyond, surpassing all others- not to be better, but to show he had the drive to learn- and now his education was in jeopardy. He tried to make sense of it all, but frankly it was all a mess. But the situation only got worse...

That Friday he was called into the conference room, where Dr. Hollis was joined with Dr. Sobrick. The two of them asked him to take a seat.

"You were given a chance to correct your mistake," began Dr. Hollis. "You were told to revise your hours to appropriately reflect your time, and you have failed to do so."

Arthur was dumbfounded. It had only been a few days; he had been given no timeframe. Now he was suddenly late in turning it in. What the hell was going on? He had only just started reviewing his hours. Was somebody out to get him? Was this a conspiracy?

She slid him an official document on letterhead. "In addition to being charged with academic dishonesty you are also being charged with several other offenses from your site supervisor."

What the hell! What was going on? Arthur snapped his neck up in surprise. Stephanie was accusing him of fraud as well? This was unbelievable! What had he done? He had followed his internship instructions to the letter, and now he was getting reprimanded for it. Surely this was a huge mistake. As he picked up the document to read it his eyes widened. Was this a joke…

The Charges

<u>Chapter 19</u>

The Accusations

In addition to being charged for falsifying his internship hours, Arthur was also being accused of four additional counts of academic dishonesty, including:

1. Taking client files outside of the facility.
2. Fabricating the number of clients.
3. Leaving the facility at midday without informing a supervisor.
4. Timeliness in reporting regularly to a supervisor.

But to add insult to injury, Stephanie had sent along her semester evaluation of Arthur, giving him a grade of 1.4 out of 5, noting that he had "disrespect for supervisors" and a "lack of empathy for clients."

Shock and disbelief hit Arthur. Was this one big joke? How was this happening? But it wasn't over yet. Stephanie also noted on her report that Arthur was bigoted and held a bias towards religious groups. Her report stated that his bias, "calls into question his competency in the area of diversity." What the hell? Where did that come from?

Dr. Hollis let it sink in. Then she spoke. "Effective immediately, you're internship is terminated. You can appeal your case, but with this list of charges I frankly wouldn't give you much of a chance. If I were you I'd cut my losses, take an F for the semester, and enroll at another institution."

Arthur ran his eyes over the charges again and again, trying to make sense of it all. He couldn't believe it. How was any of this possible? He had felt great about this place, worked hard, and now this? He couldn't make sense of it. Had the world turned upside down?

"To whom do I submit my appeal," he asked.

Dr. Hollis exchanged looks with Dr. Sobrick. "You submit your appeal to the Dean, but again you don't have much hope here." They didn't want him to fight.

But Arthur felt there was an injustice here. This was completely absurd. "I will appeal," he said.

Dr. Hollis and Dr. Sobrick shifted in their sits. "Let me also mention that I will be the one reviewing your case," she said, hoping that would deter him.

Arthur looked up, puzzled. "But, you're my advisor," he asked, noting the conflict of interest. "What if I need help preparing my appeal? Who else am I supposed to go to?"

She had him, or at least she thought she did. "I am still your advisor," she said, lying through her teeth, "but from this point forward we can no longer meet. That is until this matter is resolved."

"Well, do I get another advisor?"

"No."

"Okay, so I have no advisor to help me."

"That is correct."

"That doesn't make any sense. Shouldn't I have an advisor to help me if not you?"

"You may ask other faculty for help, but with your list of charges I don't really think anyone will want to help you. Again, I strongly encourage you to reconsider cutting your losses. It would be in your best interests."

Chapter 20

No Format Required

Dr. Hayword reported nothing but good news to the Board. She even informed them of a lowered default rating on student loans, but the new Chair still refused to hire anyone. Instead, the Chair simply thanked her for her continual hard work and devotion.

* * * * * * * *

Arthur was in disbelief. Shaken by the charges, he just sat alone in the conference room, wondering how this had happened. He was neither permitted to return to his internship nor contact anyone from it. His only chance was to appeal, but where to start was the problem: the student handbook had nothing in it regarding appeals; evidently, he was their first. In fact, the only thing the handbook stated was that he had the right to appeal. It neither stated how it should be written or in what timeframe he had to write it.

In need of clarification he went before the Dean. Bad idea. She was even less helpful than Dr. Hollis. And worse, she gave off the impression that she was hiding something.

"Thank you for seeing me," Arthur said, noting the eagle sculpture. He didn't care for it. "I hope you can help me properly prepare my appeal."

"What do you mean? Please clarify."

"Well, is there a proper format to write my appeal? I cannot find a template to use, and there's no information in the student handbook."

She crossed one arm under the other. "I understand there are very serious charges against you. So, I'm asking myself why you wish to appeal. There is clearly no chance of you exonerating yourself?"

That was perturbing to hear from a dean. "I don't believe I did anything wrong," he said, certain of his innocence.

"You may of course do as you feel is right, but I think it's important for you to know that I have the final say."

Wait, what did she mean by that? And why did she carry that tone? Arthur suddenly regretted asking her for help. Was the whole world out to get him? He tried to stay calm and collected, but this was getting ridiculous. "Is there a proper format I can use?"

"None that we have," she said, getting bored by the conversation. "So, you can write it down anyway you choose and present it to me. I will grant you ten business days to prepare it."

Ten days later, Arthur had compiled a comprehensive appeal filled with evidence. Unfortunately, it was rejected.

"Please follow the prescribed format," she said to his amazement.

"But you said there was no format."

She looked annoyed. "I am far too busy helping students who actually *earn* their grades. Now, please stop wasting my time. I have better things to do than entertain someone who cheats."

Was she serious? He had the evidence. He had the fucking evidence, and they were rejecting it because it wasn't in the correct format! And suddenly, there was a format! This was unbelievable. Flabbergasted, he walked out of her office. Stunned and in disbelief, he now sought out the prescribed template to rewrite his appeal. He was livid. He had spent the last two weeks falling behind in his course work just to write his appeal. What were they trying to do? Get him to fall behind in his course work deliberately...

<u>Chapter 21</u>

Seeking Help

Every last faculty professor politely refused to help him. Even the new librarian apologized. "I'm so sorry," she said in a soft voice. "You can look around for something that might help though." This was asinine. Nobody was going to help him, his evidence was being rejected, and he had to search an entire library on his own, because not even the librarian was going to help him. And all the while, he was falling behind in his course work as he looked for an imaginary template that presumably didn't exist until just recently.

With no one else to turn to he went to Dr. Koleman, who had heard about what was going on and felt uneasy about it; he felt particularly unsettled by Arthur's predicament. He agreed to help him, but in secrecy; frankly, he didn't trust anyone, and was becoming suspicious of the faculty. This was not how higher education was supposed to educate young people.

Arthur explained his crisis, telling him about his hours, the allegations, and how nobody was helping him. He highlighted how his hours had been approved and signed by his supervisor, but how Stephanie- for whatever reason- had taken a reverse course and given him a poor evaluation. Then he told him about how Dr. Hollis refused to be his advisor, the Dean and the template, and how he felt overwhelmed trying to search for answers in a library, not having any idea where to start. The whole thing felt unethical. It felt wrong, and frankly, he felt like there was a conspiracy against him.

"That is interesting," Dr. Koleman said, rubbing his chin. If Arthur was lying he was doing a damn good job about it, but his exasperation implied no fraud, only worry and uncertainty; Dr. Koleman suspected he was telling the truth. The question then was why was this happening.

"I honestly don't know what I've done wrong?"

"Right now, what you did is not important," Dr. Koleman said. "All that matters is what you do next. If you believe what you did was right then fight for it. Now before I help you, I'd like to share a story with you. Will that be alright?"

A. Ruben

It was not really the time for a story, but what the hell. If the man was going to help him then the last thing Arthur wanted to do was be rude.

"There once was a man pushing a car along the side of the road," Dr. Koleman said. "And not one person stopped to help him. After a long day out in the sun, a stranger pulled up alongside and offered to help him. The man graciously accepted his offer, despite the fact that the stranger wasn't very strong. Nevertheless, the two managed to push it to the nearest body shop. When they got there the man offered to pay the stranger for his troubles, but the stranger refused.

"Then something happened that was unexpected. The man who had come to help offered the driver something. Now this was unusual. We don't think of the person helping as the one offering compensation. But such is this story. The driver, not wishing to be rude, accepts, though warily. He still insisted that he should be on the one compensating, and not the other way around.

"The stranger smiled, reaching into his wallet and instead of money handed the driver a ticket, and not just any ticket. It was a movie ticket for a premier show. The driver looked at it, puzzling over it. The stranger was inviting him to

72

see a movie premier, but who was this stranger? Was he an actor? Did he buy the ticket and simply couldn't go?

"The driver didn't know. He tried to refuse the ticket, but the stranger wouldn't have it back. As it turned out, the stranger was indeed an actor, and not just any actor but a well known celebrity. Now one might think such a person might be recognized, but we forget that actors wear makeup. The driver was amazed by this. Of all the people that had ignored him the only one to stop and help him was a celebrity. Now, do you understand the morale of this story?"

Arthur shook his head.

"Well, I want you to remember this story. Can you do that for me? Because, perhaps one day you may understand. Alright, let's start formatting your appeal."

Chapter 22

No Way Out

In addition to Dr. Hollis, Dr. Sobrick, the Dean and Stephanie, the recently hired Vice President of Administration also began reviewing his case. Suddenly, the conspiracy was enlarging. Little did Arthur realize the nuclear implosion that his debacle would ignite.

* * * * * * * * *

Thirty-five pages and three weeks later, Arthur submitted his appeal to the Dean who subsequently turned it over to the investigative committee headed by none other than Dr. Hollis. Just as before he was told the template was wrong; he was informed he had used an older template, and needed to redo it using the updated format. It was total BS.

"Please understand that our time is far too valuable to be expended on incomplete documentation," Dr. Hayword told him, getting upset by his continual persistence. But five weeks later he resubmitted it again. Now for the third time.

By now the second semester was over, and he had fallen seriously behind in his course work. To leverage him to stop appealing he was given no extensions on his assignments, no office hours to meet with his professors, and issued a letter stating his second semester credits would reflect "No Credit." Clearly, there was an effort to get him to quit, but he was too stubborn for that: when that didn't work he was simply turned away from the registrar's office. He wasn't allowed to register for classes for the third semester.

How could an institution forbid him from registering for classes? Well, it was entirely due to the Vice President of Admissions, who was now onboard with the conspirators, and she made it very clear that Arthur was not to receive any form of student services help, including the registrar. When he made an appointment to meet with her she leveled with him very bluntly. "The semester is now over, and all grades are in. I don't see why you wish to continue given your failing marks. I would strongly encourage you to exit the program."

Three failed appeal tries. His grades marked as no credit. Staff refusing to help him. No extensions. No registering for additional classes to make up for the no credit. He was waist deep in a shit creek, and to add insult to injury the other students kept their distance from him.

Whatever trouble he was in they wanted no part of; no doubt he had brought it upon himself. During lectures, he often found himself seated alone. If his world was in chaos now it was just beginning to slide downhill.

Chapter 23

Strangers on the Side

With the Board under the new Chair now declining to hire any further staff or faculty, Dr. Hayword took a different course, expanding growth through the responsibilities of her staff. This was not received well, as it meant more work with no additional pay. So to win support of this, she started making promises she couldn't keep.

* * * * * * * *

In the meanwhile, several directors at the facility began asking about Arthur's whereabouts. He hadn't been seen in days and they were concerned; by now they were accustomed to his daily inquires and felt an absence in their day without it. Yet when they approached Stephanie she refused to elaborate, remarking only that he was no longer interning there.

"If that will be all then you are dismissed," she said, coldly pointing to the door. They were already troubled by her policies, but the fact that she seemed to be holding back from them deeply bothered them. And so they turned to the other interns at the facility, probing for whatever information they could learn about his whereabouts. None were entirely sure of what had transpired, but shared what they knew.

"I see him here and there," said one female intern. "So I think he's still in the program."

"But why doesn't he come here if he goes to class?"

She just shrugged her shoulders. "I'm not really sure."

"Any idea why he would be missing class?"

"Sorry, I'm not sure about that either. It's not something anyone is really talking about."

"Why do you say that?" asked a director.

"Well, none of the professors are talking about it. In fact, it's really hush-hush. So, either nobody is saying anything or it's just no big deal. I mean this is graduate school after all. Some make it, and some don't."

But something didn't add up. Arthur never seemed to be the struggling type. At least, that was the impression the directors got. After all, he was the only intern who came regularly four to five times a week. He put forth the effort and it had showed; he had received compliments from both clients as well as other staff, who he had taken advice from; his dedication to his studies was as apparent as his passion to learn, so to believe he was failing was a hard pill to swallow.

Determined to get to the bottom of it, several directors approached Yolanda. The two interacted almost daily. So, if anyone knew something it was she. Unfortunately, she was just as baffled as they were.

"Something isn't right here," she said. And with that she began her own investigation.

<u>Chapter 24</u>

Restrictions

Composed of corporate executives and financiers, the Board assessed the institute's growth with a vigilant eye. Nonetheless, Dr. Hayword still tried to push for expansion despite continual rejection. "There is no sense in putting the cart before the horse," the Chair said. "Thank you for your time. That will be all."

* * * * * * * *

Now under the scrutiny of the Board, Dr. Hayword did her best to hide Arthur from them. Any mention of him publicly was prohibited. Any assistance in his appeal was forbidden. He was granted very specific times to meet with his professors for course inquiries, but no office hours, only a fixed amount of time after class. Furthermore, Arthur was warned against asking for anymore help on his appeal.

He was restricted to the lecture halls and library only, but certain sections of the library he was barred from, including the legal shelves. Moreover, he was permitted only one hour per day in the library, and that hour had to be supervised by a staff member. In addition, that hour was given a very specific timeframe, which not surprisingly coincided with a class of his. So, it was either go to class or use the library.

Furthermore, he was forbidden to speak of his appeal to anyone under penalty of expulsion. He was warned against entering the student union. He was warned against lounging in student areas, where other students mingled and socialized. He was not allowed to go there on orders of the Dean. He was instructed on what times he was permitted to be on campus and when to leave: as soon as class was over he could talk with his professors for his allotted time- not about the appeal, but only coursework. Then he was to leave the campus. Failure to leave would result in charges of trespassing, and possible arrest.

He was permitted to use the computer lab, but again limited to one hour per day. Although he had his own computer at his apartment, he was not permitted to check out any resources from the library, or print off anything from the computer lab that might pertain to his appeal. Everything he printed off was to be inspected by a staff member. Any abuse or infraction would revoke his one-hour privilege.

But for all the restrictions, Arthur did get help. The librarian, who was under strict orders to observe him and enforce the time, decided to be lax. She simply forgot to look at the clock, giving him a wink. She could see he was trying, and something in her gut told her he was innocent. When Dr. Koleman met with him they worked behind closed doors. And one of the admissions advisors, under the Vice-President of Admissions, blatantly ignored orders not to help him and did the opposite. She later quit, appalled by the scandal when it finally came to light.

Chapter 25

Competency

Dr. Sobrick often had lunch with Stephanie, and they always had a good laugh together. They were close friends. Very close.

* * * * * * * *

In addition to being his academic advisor and chairing the investigation against him, Dr. Hollis performed his end-of-the-semester evaluation. Not surprisingly, her evaluation matched Stephanie's. In it, she too pointed out Arthur's clear apparent disregard for authority by noting how he "openly demonstrated disrespect." This was in reference to an incident when he had gone into her office to wait for her. She accused him of entering without permission. That was a lie.

She had told him to wait inside while she retrieved something off the printer.

"He also lacks an adequate level of understanding of how he impacts others," she further noted, again making referencing to a time in which he had asked her for help. Evidently, his request for help was intrusive.

Then she noted his bias, supporting what Stephanie had written. She said he "failed to accept diversity by addressing certain staff more preferentially than others." And by this she meant he ignored some staff while speaking with others. Which was an interesting way to view the gag order issued by the Dean to all faculty, not to help or address Arthur. The only one who violated that had been Dr. Koleman.

Dr. Hollis gave Arthur's evaluation a 1 out of 5, adding that he lacked "sensitivity to issues of power, oppression and privilege." She really did dive into sheep's skin. Lastly, she called into question his apparent inability to discern dangerous situations, noting that her discussions with him "reflect a markedly low level of awareness concerning the potential for harm by a client to self, or to others." That was interesting. If this were even true then how did she know about his clients unless someone like Stephanie told her.

After all, isn't medical information supposed to be confidential by federal law?

Chapter 26

Discerning Facts

Dr. Hayword regularly inquired after Dr. Koleman's reaction towards her institute. Like a hostess to a special guest, she looked after him with care, giving him a large office and putting whatever resources he needed at his disposal. All that mattered was being accredited.

* * * * * * * * *

Yolanda inquired after interns, investigating like a private detective. As she pieced facts together the truth began to unfold. It was one thing to terminate an employee, but Arthur had been a promising young student who hadn't even started his career; he neither had real world experience nor a fledging résumé to fall back on. And what had been his crime?

She had come to appreciate him for who he was, inquisitive, lively, humble and eager to learn. He had a friendly disposition that was inviting, and when others spoke he listened. "Honey, you're in the right profession," she had once said to him, ingratiating his concern for others.

Now upon learning of the allegations against him she gathered as many directors as she could and barged into the CEO's office. This time Stephanie had crossed the line; her policies and beliefs had been tolerated, but there was no excuse for this malicious act. Placing the facts on his desk, she and a handful of directors threatened to quit that day if Stephanie was not terminated.

Taken aback by this sudden intrusion into his office, the CEO asked for an explanation. He got one. In addition to hearing the charges against Arthur he was also shown duplicates of his time sheets, and right there on each page was Stephanie's signature.

"True, but he could have forged his hours," the CEO replied. "It's not Stephanie's fault if he is being fraudulent."

That was a good point, except for a variety of reasons. The first being that Arthur didn't just submit his hours. He actually had to sit down with Stephanie and review them before she signed off. So, there was one-on-one interaction.

A. Ruben

In addition, the timesheets were then sent over to Yolanda's department where they were verified for billing or non-billing purposes, and then filed away. In Arthur's case, he had always made a personal effort to get a copy of his hours each week from her. He didn't have to. Other interns didn't. But Arthur wanted a copy of his hours for his records, and there was nothing illegal about that. Moreover, Yolanda said, he had asked her if he was filling it out correctly, always making sure so that his hours would be accepted by the institute.

The CEO scratched his face. Yolanda was putting herself in harm's way. If Arthur had been fraudulent then Yolanda had just admitted to being an accomplice. But if that were true what was in it for her? He couldn't think of anything. So, either Yolanda was waiving her 5th Amendment and admitting guilt if Arthur truly was guilty, or Stephanie had lied. He was unsure. But then the odds tipped in favor of Arthur when Yolanda presented the next bit of evidence:

How could Arthur have lied about his clients when Stephanie issued them to him every week? Even if he had made them up and tried to slide it through it was Yolanda's staff that, again, verified client data for billing or non-billing purposes. If the client was falsified she would have known, and then why on earth would she be vouching for him? That would make no sense.

"Are you absolutely sure about these facts," the CEO asked, weighing the heavy decision before him.

"The facts don't lie, even if she did," she said.

Chapter 27

Unearthing the Truth

Arthur preferred to spend as little time at his apartment as possible. In addition to the drive-by shootings his contract also strictly forbad a number of things, one of which was prostitutes.

* * * * * * * *

Arthur had fallen so far behind in his studies that he had no choice now but to leave the program. It was depressing. He was downcast and exhausted from his endeavors. He had tried to exonerate himself, but to no avail. Each of his appeals had been rejected for trivial reasons; the evidence wasn't even looked at. The Dean was right. She had final say, and frankly, she didn't even bother reading his appeal.

Refusing to Grow 3

And so, defeated, he packed up his apartment. Despairing over having student loans with nothing to show for it he felt down on his luck. But just as he loaded the last box into the moving van he received an unexpected phone call. It was from another intern at the facility.

"Have you heard?" she asked, excitedly.

"Heard what?" He didn't know what she was talking about; he had been ostracized by the student body, ignored by staff except for Dr. Koleman, and had his educational path set back by this debacle.

"She got fired!"

"Who? Who got fired?"

He couldn't believe it. Stephanie had been dismissed on charges of unprofessionalism, and with that everything was coming to light, from her racial policies to her fraudulent allegations of Arthur: none of the evidence corroborated with her evaluation of him. He had done everything by the book, which led to a string of inquiry. Suddenly, there were more questions than answers.

Why did Stephanie submit a false report of Arthur?

Why did Stephanie lie, and submit false allegations?

What was her reason for such unprofessionalism?

The facility launched its own investigation into why Stephanie had defrauded Arthur. Frankly, it made no sense why, as his supervisor, that she did it. And as they dug deeper the facility kept coming back to the institute: Stephanie's once secret relationship with Dr. Sobrick; Dr. Sobrick's role on the investigative committee against Arthur; Dr. Hollis and her role as chairing the investigative committee; the conflict of interest of Dr. Hollis as both chair of the investigative committee and as advisor to Arthur; the several appeals Arthur had made; the trivial reasons for why his appeals were rejected; Dr. Koleman's help, but no other staff; the gag order issued by the Dean; and then why Dr. Hayword had tried to hide it from the Board.

"It's all coming out now," the intern said.

The Board was suddenly now aware and demanded an explanation for the secrecy and the lies; horrified by the appalling revelation of a possible scandal they instantly conducted an investigation of their own. All at once, faculty, exposed the details. Too astonished to speak, the Chair demanded all the names and parties involved. Although it was too late to save Arthur the reputation of the institute could still be salvaged, and as the facts came to light, he could not believe what was being unearthed.

The Dean tried to vindicate herself but to no avail when Dr. Koleman abruptly informed the Board of what he had witnessed. "I live with the decisions I make, and what I saw here was a tragedy." His decision to refuse the institute its advanced accreditation spelled the doom for anything Dr. Hayword tried to assert.

Chapter 28

Epilogue

Dr. Koleman returned home, disappointed in the constitution of the institute. It had had promise, but its values deeply conflicted with what he considered to be the core principal of education, that learning is foremost above everything else. And so, as he boarded the plane, he thought back on Arthur. He hoped the young man had remembered his story and silently wished him all the best. He had been the driver in the story, but this time he had been the celebrity helping another in need.

Meanwhile, Dr. Hollis filled Dr. Koleman's role as the chair for graduate studies, but was required to report regularly to a member of the Board. Her involvement had been particularly deplorable given her evaluation and especially her contradicting role as both his academic advisor as well as the chair of his investigation.

On the other hand, Dr. Sobrick was at first vindicated of any wrongdoing. In addition to being allowed to continue presenting at conferences he was also promoted to Director of Clinical Training for graduate studies. Unfortunately for him, when his secret relationship with Stephanie came to light he was exposed and resigned.

Following revelations of the scandal, a number of other faculty and staff immediately resigned, and although new ones were hired the scarring remained visible. Despite their best intentions to repair the damage, the Board could not ignore the fact that their attempt to receive advanced accreditation was denied; that didn't come until ten years later when they tried again and were finally accredited.

Dr. Hayword was stripped of her role as Dean, but allowed to serve as part of the faculty. A year later however, she was demoted to associate faculty and then asked to serve as just a "consultant." Finally, she was altogether removed from the institute's list. But then unexpectedly she was asked back and promoted to the role of President. Oddly enough, her promotion led to another round of resignations as faculty numbers suddenly dropped by 57% and staff numbers exponentially.

And as for Arthur, he finished his studies at another institute, receiving half a dozen letters of commendation from his mentors. Despite the onset of an economic recession and a difficulty securing a teaching job, he nevertheless kept his chin up and was determined to face any new storm with resolve. He wanted to be a teacher, but when that proved difficult he took a job in sales…

9 780975 459041